A Mother of Faith

by

Dan Cotrone

ACKNOWLEDGMENTS

A warm thank you to:

Mom and Dad for allowing me to see the faithfulness of the Lord in your lives, so that I might, as a result, see it in mine. Thank you for the legacy of faith and the foundation of truth...

My wonderful wife, Janet, for your devoted love and support. You have faithfully stood by my side and held up my arms with your faith. Thank you for the encouragement, the laughter, and even the tears. I love you...

Our beautiful children, Daniel, Denise, David, and Deanine, for many years of joy. You are all proof of Mom's faith and prayers. Thank you for allowing the Lord to use you as He has. I am blessed beyond measure...

My brothers and sisters, Donna, Angie, Rock, Frankie, Anthony, and Kathy, and your families for allowing Mom's faith to work in your lives. Thank you for the joyous memories and the experiences we have shared together...

The Village of Faith congregation for your receptive hearts and your encouragement on writing this book. You have heard some of these stories enough times to tell them on your own! May you continue to receive life and faith from them...

Cristina Giovanniello, Donna Scuderi, Karen Warren, Lynn Rowlynson, and Pat Maltempo for your help on the manuscript in its early stages; and Alece Ronzino, who miraculously took it and ran with it until it was completed. Thank you for your hard work and the wonderful way you captured my heart on these pages...

The Lord for allowing me this opportunity to present my family to the world, so that You might be glorified. Thank you for Your perfect faithfulness and unending love. To God be the glory!

DEDICATION

In loving memory of Dr. Lester Sumrall, a dear friend and co-laborer in the Kingdom. Dr. Sumrall was a tremendous blessing to me and my ministry over the years. He always encouraged me to continue striving for the best and to never give up; and he was the one who really pushed me to write this book about my mom.

They were kindred spirits, Dr. Sumrall and my mom. They both were tough, strong, take-charge people with a bold faith. They knew how to listen for the voice of the Lord and then to act on what He said; and as a result, both their lives were filled beyond measure with the blessings of God.

I am encouraged to know that Dr. Sumrall and my mom are together in Glory...

FOREWORD

◯◯

Never in all our years have we ever read a book of such beautiful, simple faith as <u>A Mother of Faith</u>. We are blessed to know the entire Cotrone family, including the mother and father written about in this book. The whole family has one of the most incredible family relationships with each other and some of the most tremendous family love we have ever seen. What an example they are to other families! After ministering in their church we have often said how we wish that all families had the same love for each other that this incredible Italian family has.

<u>A Mother of Faith</u> displays one of the most unusual, simple kinds of faith, but it is a faith greater than that of any other person we have ever known. When Caterina heard from God she knew that was it, and she never questioned Him one single time! It would be so wonderful if all of us could walk in that kind of faith at all times. Caterina never wavered once what God wanted her to do! She

never vacillated or backed down regardless of what the reports were from other people.

We believe that those who read this will discover a tremendous challenge to your own faith, regardless of where your faith level is. Sometimes we need to go back to the beautiful, simple faith that Caterina Cotrone had. To know her was to love her. To know her family was to love to love them, and that includes the entire family all the way down to the grandchildren.

It is our distinct privilege and honor to be able to recommend this book to anyone who wants to increase their faith or who wants to draw their family closer to them in the relationship that God intended for families to have.

Charles and Frances Hunter

Having known Pastor Dan Cotrone for a number of years, I was delighted when he asked me to write a foreword for this book. I had the pleasure of meeting Dan's mother and father several years ago, and I can testify to their sincere love for Jesus and their family.

Dan's Mom was an inspiration, and always welcomed me with a big hug and kisses on both sides of my face. She always made me feel like one of the family. Dan often shared with me the many miracles that his mom had experienced; and after reading this book, it brought back to me some wonderful memories.

Anyone who reads <u>A Mother of Faith</u> will be inspired and encouraged to believe God no matter how impossible your circumstances may seem. There is something special about a mother's faith. God truly honors it and as you read this enjoyable account of a mother who dared to believe God, you will become more and more convinced that all things are possible to those who believe.

Jerry Savelle

INTRODUCTION

This book has been many years in the making. Various attempts were made, over a period of about fifteen years, to accurately capture the life of my mother on paper. These stories, incidents, and memories are things which have burned within my heart since childhood. They branded within me a resolute faith in God, as I saw Him prove Himself strong on behalf of my mother and our entire family. This book is an attempt to express to you the simplicity and power of my mother's faith in hopes that *your* faith is built up as a result.

My prayer is that you walk away from this book encouraged. I pray that your eyes will be opened and your heart softened as you read, so that you may *"taste and see that the Lord is good."* (Psalm 34:8) As you read about the things the Lord has done in my family as a result of my mom's prayers of faith, remember that *"God does not show favoritism."* (Romans 2:11) Be sure that if He did it for my mother—just an "ordinary" mom and housewife—He will do the same for you!

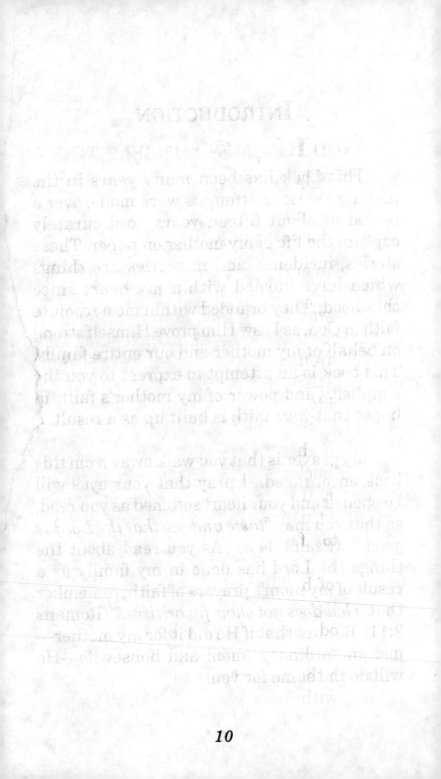

Chapter One

GOD REVEALS HIMSELF TO CATERINA BUSCIETI

∽

It was an early summer morning in 1923 in Calabria, Italy. Eight-year old Caterina Buscieti was taking a walk down to the well to get a bucket of water, as she often did. This particular morning she enjoyed the walk, appreciating the quiet serenity of the countryside.

When she arrived at the well, Caterina took her bucket and, as always, lowered it in. However, this morning she was not concentrating on what she was doing and, leaning too far into the well to retrieve the full bucket, she fell in. Instinctively, she thought of her father and the prayers they often said together as a family; and she cried out to God. Suddenly she felt strong hands grab her. Miraculously she found herself sitting on the ground beside the well, totally unhurt, with nobody else around. It was a notable miracle from God.

This is but one of the many miracles in the life of my mother, a woman who prayed and received answers to her prayers as simply as the Bible tells us we can. Mom experienced the miraculous from a very young age. She had a very spiritual sense of the Lord, more so than the rest of her family. Her father was a wonderful example to her. He faithfully walked an hour-and-a-half to church and back every Sunday; and he prayed with his family for at least one hour every night. However, Mom wanted to know more about the things of the Lord.

She would often ask her parents questions about the Lord; but they were not able to answer her or explain the things she asked about. When the local priests would come to the village, Mom would try to get their attention so that she could talk to them about the things of God. They always brushed her aside as "just a young girl". They appeared too busy to answer her questions, and she was never taken seriously; so Mom sought the Lord for herself.

Although she did not have a Bible, and did

not know what the Word of God says, she believed that God would always protect her and provide for her. She knew there was "another force" that was against her, trying to hurt her, but she always relied on the Lord to see her through. And He always did!

Once when Mom was four years old, she ran out of the house to meet her father who was returning home with the cows. A bull charged her and caught her in its horns, hurling her on her back. One of her legs was broken, and she wore a cast for forty days. When the doctors removed it, the bone had set incorrectly, leaving her leg four inches too short. Without anesthetic, the doctors broke her leg again and put her in another cast. This time her leg healed perfectly. Again God had come through with a miraculous intervention!

When Mom was twelve, she fell out of a cherry tree. However, she described her landing as though she had fallen on a soft cushion, and she was totally unhurt. There was no natural way the hard ground could have felt so soft. It was just another reminder to Mom of the angels all around her. *"For He will command His angels concerning you to guard you in all your ways."* (Psalm 91:11) It was another example of God's faithfulness to her.

Chapter Two

THE FAMILY BEGINS

❧

The Lord gave Mom a wonderful spirit, and a servant's heart. As a young girl, she always did her daily chores joyfully, singing God's faithfulness. She enjoyed preparing the meals and serving her family, and always did so with a song in her heart and a smile on her face.

Throughout her adolescent years, Mom's faith in the Lord continued to grow. She began to cling to spiritual things even more. The things of the Lord were always present in her heart and mind to strengthen and encourage her when things were hard. She always knew that God would see her through.

God had placed in Mom's heart the assurance that He would one day send to her someone who would love her very dearly. She knew that someday she would leave all that she was accustomed to and travel to a better place that would be her real home, where she would be surrounded by her own family.

When Mom was seventeen years old, one of her brothers who lived in the States sent her a picture of a friend of his. She had never met him, but immediately fell in love with the handsome Italian American with the friendly brown eyes. Even though it became somewhat of a family joke, she believed that God would send Antonio Cotrone to Italy.

Antonio was living in New York City. He had grown up on the Lower East Side, very much looked up to by his five younger siblings. He was a diligent, hard worker, and he was his brothers' and sisters' protector and provider. He loved people, had many friends, and was highly respected. Antonio feared nothing. One time he was getting a shave in the barber shop when someone ran in yelling, *"Tony! Tony! They're beating up on your brother!"* He ran out of the shop and sure enough, there was his brother Don getting beaten up in the street. Antonio ran down the street with shaving cream all over his face, and knocked the guys out that were beating up his brother—with one punch! With that, he was nicknamed, "One-Punch Tony".

Antonio had his pick, if he wanted, of attractive women. He was good looking, athletic, and strong. He also owned a car, which was a stamp of success back then. But, still, as several women chased him, he opted to wait for the right woman, the perfect mate. One summer, four years after Mom had seen his picture, Antonio visited Italy with his father. The rest is history. Mom and Dad had a brief courtship and an old-fashioned Italian wedding. Then Dad returned to the United States and waited for Mom to obtain the necessary papers in order to join him in America.

Eighteen months later Mom was finally able to go. It was traumatic for her to leave her home, her country, and everything she held dear; and she spent the seven-day boat ride in bed with stomach sickness. She comforted herself by thinking about God's goodness. She knew she was in the Lord's hands and that He was leading her and guiding her. She thought of her new husband waiting patiently for her in the States. God's peace calmed her fears; and she knew she would be all right.

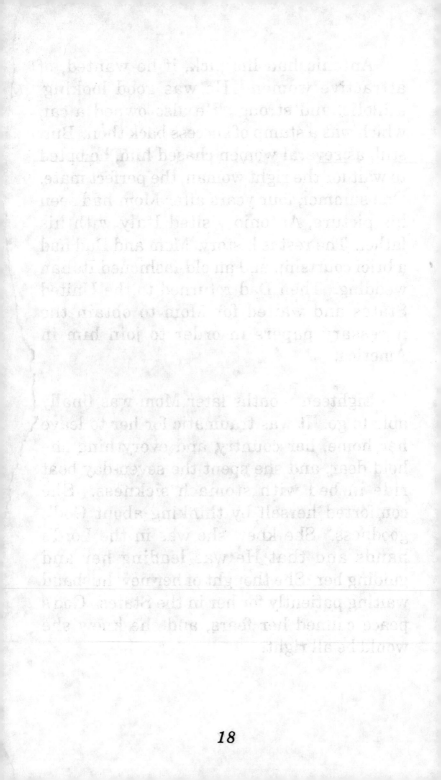

18

Chapter Three

GOD ALSO LIVES ON THE LOWER EAST SIDE

∽

When she arrived in New York, Mom quickly realized that America was not the "land of milk and honey" as she had thought. She and Dad lived in a tiny apartment on the top floor of a tenant building on Ludlow Street. Mom did not see the hills of Calabria anymore; instead she only saw tall, crowded buildings that shook every time a car drove by on the cobblestone streets below. She was terrified of the noises from the street and the shaking of the apartment; and she was overwhelmed by all the shouting because she could not understand English. Mom became so overcome by fear, that she lost her joy and her happiness. The devil came and stole the life from her spirit; and Mom became very sick. All the fear, loneliness, and depression sapped the life right out of her, and she became bedridden.

For months, Mom lay in bed, unable to do housework or cook or do anything at all. Dad's family tried to comfort and encourage her; but nothing they did seemed to help. Their words did not do it for her. But one day, Mom started to talk with the Lord; and she asked Him, *"Did You bring me here to stay in bed and be sick?"*

When He said, *"No,"* Mom replied, *"Then why am I stuck in this bed?"*

The Lord spoke to her heart, *"Get out of bed."*

Mom argued, *"I'm sick; I can't get out of bed."*

Again she heard the Lord say to her, *"Get out of bed."*

The Lord showed Mom that the same God that was with her in Galabria was with her on the Lower East Side of Manhattan. For months, many people tried to minister to her, but their words didn't help; but as soon as God spoke, life came back to her limbs, her mind, and her spirit. Nothing happened until she opened herself up to speak to the Lord; and He was there waiting for her. *"Are you done with them now? Are you done asking people to help you? Now can I talk to you? I am with you. I have always been with you. How do you think you got here?"*

Mom's faith rose up as she realized that God was still with her, and she got out of bed. Instantly, the Lord touched her, and she was healed. She felt the strength of God flow into her body like never before, and she began to straighten up the house. She cleaned the entire place, and then started to prepare dinner.

I can picture my Dad coming home from work that evening. They lived on the top floor; so instead of counting six flights of stairs, Dad would run up to the roof, and then run back down one flight to their floor. I can hear my Dad saying to himself, *"What do I smell?! Smells like food cooking! That can't be coming from my house!"* Dad opened the door and looked around. He was shocked to see the apartment spotless and Mom setting the food on the table. *"Oh my God, Katie; what happened?!"*

"Shutup!" Mom answered in her typical way. *"God talked to me. He came with me*

from Calabria to here, and I had forgotten. But He took care of me. No one else could; but God did it!"

Mom had allowed God's Word to enter her spirit, and they produced not death nor sickness, but life, health, and peace. Jesus said in John 6:63, *"The words that I speak unto you, they are spirit, and they are life."*

Mom knew that her strength came from the Lord. She knew that He was her sustenance, her all in all. Her prayer life increased tremendously as she wholeheartedly devoted herself to the Lord and to spending time with Him.

Chapter Four

LIFE IN NEW YORK CITY

Mom was completely restored, filled with joy, and ready to begin her new life and family. She and Dad had four children while they lived in the City: Donna (short for Dominica), myself, Angie, and Rocco. They were always striving for something better for our growing family. God had placed it in her heart to always want the best; and if she saw a chance to move the family to nicer surroundings, she took it. Mom was always scouting around for a better place, and when she would find it she would call to Dad, in her proverbial way, *"Come on, Tony! It's time to move on!"* So they moved five times in five years, and every apartment was nicer than the last. Sometimes they moved to an apartment that was simply a floor closer to ground level. Other times the move was to an apartment that had its own bathroom, rather than one in the hall to be shared with the other tenants. Each move meant increase; and each move was a step up for us.

No matter where we were though, we always knew that our parents loved us and wanted the best for us. Dad always made sure that he spent quality time with us, in spite of his long hours at work; and we never had to worry about not having enough. We could always count on Dad to provide for us. I will never forget one time when I was a small boy, I was sitting on the stoop outside our apartment in the city when my Dad came home from work. When he asked me how I was doing, I told him that I had not eaten anything and that I was hungry.

"I didn't feel like running all the way up the stairs to our apartment to get something to eat."

Dad pointed to the deli next door. *"Why didn't you go buy yourself something?"*

"I don't have any money."

My Dad gave me money to go buy something to eat. He told me to feel free to get myself something from the deli anytime I was hungry, and that he would pay for it when he got home from work. He said that I never had to worry about not eating. So, every day from then until we moved to Brooklyn, I went into the deli and got a ham and cheese hero; and ate it on the stoop of 125 Elizabeth Street, enjoying every bite. Dad would always go in after work and pay for my lunch. Never would he question any of my purchases. He truly cared for the needs of his children! *"If you, then, though you are evil, know how to give good gifts to your children, how much more will your Father in heaven give good gifts to those who ask Him."* (Matthew 7:11)

Chapter Five

"Come On, Tony! It's Time To Move On!"

∞

After living in the city for five years, another move was in the making. Without having told Dad, Mom had managed to save enough money for a small down payment on a house. The thought of moving into a house must have been God-inspired, because for so many people, living in an apartment is a life-style; that is difficult to break out of. Yet Mom, through the power of God, had a vision. She had a vision of a better life for her family, and she and Dad worked toward seeing that vision come to pass.

"Come on, Tony! It's time to move on!" They purchased a four thousand-dollar house on Monroe Street in the Bushwick section of Brooklyn. How Mom had been able to save the money with four young mouths to feed is difficult to imagine. Yet she did, and once again Mom and Dad's vision for a better life allowed

us to expand our borders and prosper in a new home: a home that was all ours.

Not too long after we moved to Brooklyn, as Mom expected her fifth child, she began to feel run down. The doctors said the situation was serious that she would need a miracle in order for her pregnancy to come to full term. Rather than believe what she had heard, Mom chose to believe the Lord.

Someone told her about St. Francis Cabrini Church in the Bronx, where miracles were known to take place. Mom and Dad took us all down there to believe God for a miracle. When we got there, Mom knelt down and, in a simple prayer, promised God that if He would bless her she would name the child after Mother Cabrini.

On January 8, 1948, Frank, Mom and Dad's fifth child, was born, full term and perfectly healthy. A miracle child, my brother was named Francis Xavier Cotroneo, after Francis Xavier Cabrini.

Within that same year, Anthony was born, December 23. Mom needed the power of God more than ever, and she needed spiritual support. One of Mom's friends told her about a good church in the Flatbush section of Brooklyn. Her friend took her one Sunday, and as soon as she walked into the building, she knew it was to be her church. Reverend Montemarano, a stern, middle-aged, Italian man with broken English spoke with Mom. He shared with her the importance, and the power, of prayer. He also drew up a diet for Mom that would increase her strength. *"They that wait upon the Lord shall renew their strength; they shall mount up with wings as eagles; they shall run, and not be weary; and they shall walk, and not faint."* (Isaiah 40:31)

Chapter Six

THE SUPERNATURAL INTERVENTION OF GOD

∽

Early one morning in the summer of 1948, when I was eight years old, my mom asked me to help Dad paint the kitchen chairs. However, my friends were playing in the street outside our house, so I went out to join them instead. We wanted to play boxball, but the ice truck owned by the father of one of my friends was in our way. So the man's son decided to move it. Figuring we could get a free ride, we all grabbed the metal bars on the outside of the truck. However, when the truck jerked into reverse, I fell off and the truck's back two wheels rolled over both my legs, crushing them.

One of the older boys carried me back to the house. I was in tremendous pain. Hearing what happened, Mom fell to her knees in front of the house. She began praying very loudly, crying and pleading with God on my behalf.

She never looked at me but directed her focus and her prayers to heaven. I have never forgotten how Mom looked away from the circumstances and focused immediately on the Lord.

I was rushed to Bushwick Hospital, but when the doctors saw the seriousness of my legs, I was transferred to Kings County Hospital where specialists would be better able to help me. They placed both legs in a cast from hip to toe; and I stayed in the hospital for a week. The doctors were very negative about the situation. They said that my legs would take a very long time to heal, and when they did, they might never be the same again. They might not be straight and I might never be able to walk again. Mom had prayed with her pastor regarding the situation; and he said that he believed I would be totally healed in one month. Mom told me what he said, believing it to be a word from God; and I too, believed that God would heal me.

Two weeks after my release from the hospital, I went to the doctor for a checkup. X-rays were taken, and I was told to return in a month. However, the very next week was exactly one month after my accident, so we went back to the hospital. The month was up and we were believing that I was healed. Mom and I asked the doctor to take another set of x-rays. He refused, saying it was impossible for any major changes to have occurred already. However, because both Mom and I insisted, he reluctantly took the x-rays. He came back and said that he would have to take another set. The x-rays had shown my legs perfectly whole, which could not be right, so he needed to redo the x-rays. So another set of x-rays were taken and the doctor compared them with the x-rays taken one week earlier during my checkup visit. He called in other doctors to take a look —they could not believe their eyes! The new x-rays showed that my bones were totally healed and that my legs were fine! As the doctors scratched their heads wondering how this could be, Mom explained to them that God had healed my legs.

The cast was removed, and I went home. However my legs were extremely skinny —like two sticks—and I was unable to put any weight on them. If the slightest bit of weight was put on them, I felt as though I was being electrocuted, sharp pains running up and down my legs. Mom received insight from the Lord on how I could strengthen my legs and she had Dad build me a tricycle. I would ride it up and down the block working and strengthening my legs. The bike was handmade and wobbly, and would often fall over if I turned quickly, so I frequently fell off. I would have to drag myself over to the bike and somehow drag myself back onto it. It was very hard and painful for me; but each time I fell off, it was that much easier for me to get back on.

After a few weeks, my legs were strong enough for me to walk with crutches; and only two months after the accident, I was up and walking on my own again, as healthy and strong as any other boy my age. I was able to run and keep up with the best of them, just as I had done before. I truly saw it as a miracle. I knew that God had intervened in my life as a result of Mom's faith; and I knew that the Lord would always answer our prayers if we would step out and act on His Word.

"He keepeth all his bones: not one of them is broken." (Psalm 34:20)

Chapter Seven

ANTHONY'S MIRACULOUS RETURN FROM VIETNAM

∞

Mom was always concerned with Anthony. She felt he needed extra prayer and attention. When Anthony was just 19 years old and at the height of the Vietnam War, Anthony was drafted in the army. Mom was very upset and worried about Anthony going in the army and being away from home for the first time. With constant television bulletins on the Vietnam War casualties, Mom knew she had to pray more than ever for Anthony's safe return. So, Anthony went to Vietnam; and Mom became even more serious about praying for him, the youngest of her four sons. She prayed fervently for Anthony; and would get the entire family together every day to pray for him as well. And the Lord in His faithfulness answered the prayers of our family.

After graduating basic training, Anthony was transferred to Fort Knox, Kentucky where he graduated in the top ten from tank training school. Eleven months later, Anthony was promoted to sergeant and then sent overseas to Vietnam. While many of his friends—and even his lieutenant—died around him in the war, the angels of God that encamped about Anthony as a result of Mom's prayers, kept him from harm. He was only in Vietnam a few days when his tank unit came under heavy fire, and the tank alongside his was hit, killing all the soldiers inside it. Anthony helped carry the dead soldiers to his tank until they could be safely evacuated.

Anthony returned home with two Purple Hearts for wounds received in action, the Bronze Star Medal, the Conspicuous Service State of New York Medal, and the Combat Infantry Badge. Mom's prayers—and the prayers of the entire family—were answered, and Anthony came back home safe and sound. The Lord is true to His Word: *"The angel of the Lord encamps around those who fear Him, and He delivers them."* (Psalm 34:7)

Chapter Eight

ASK AND YOU WILL RECEIVE

When Rock (Rocco) was 22 years old, the government started to move up the draft age for the Vietnam War. They started taking 19 year olds, then 20 year olds, and then 21 year olds. He started to get worried; so he asked Mom, *"Mom, are you praying?"* And she told him in her broken English, *"Don't worry. I'm praying. You will be all right. When I prayed, God told me that you no go to Vietnam."*

Then Rock received a letter from the draft board on a Friday, telling him to report for active duty the following Monday. So he took the letter to Mom and showed her and she said to him, *"God told me you no go! Trust God!"*

That afternoon Rock received a call from my sister Angie. She told him that she did not want to get his hopes up or anything, but her girlfriend's husband Harvey had just gotten out of the National Guard. He was willing to take Rock to speak with the Captain of the company that he had just gotten out of, and maybe they could arrange something so that he could join the National Guard (which would mean that he would not have to go to Vietnam). Rock got very excited; and when he told Mom she said, *"See! I told you!"*

So that night, Harvey took Rock to the Jamaica Armory. As they walked up to the Captain's office on the third floor, Rock was praising the Lord and thanking Him for His goodness and His faithfulness. Harvey introduced Rock to the Captain, explained about Rock having to report for duty on Monday, and asked if there was anyway he could get him into the National Guard. The Captain said he was sorry, but he had a list of 2,000 men who wanted to get into the National Guard to escape going to Vietnam; but they already had forty men over the amount they were supposed to have.

As Rock walked back down the same stairs he had walked up praising God, he was saying to himself, *"What happened? How did Mom miss this? Oh my God..."*

When they got down to the bottom floor, Harvey asked Rock to wait a few minutes so he could say hi to some friends. So Rock stood to the side just waiting, until he noticed some men working on a truck. They had the canvas off the top and they were hammering in some two by fours. Being a carpenter by trade, Rock was interested in finding out what they were doing, so he went over and inquired. The men told him that they were building an office in the truck for the commander-in-chief of the New York National Guard. It was going to be fully equipped with a bathroom, bar, heating, air conditioning, etc. Rock told them he was a carpenter and gave them a few ideas on how to cut the lumber and do some of the work. When Rock explained to the men that he had come to try to enlist, but he couldn't get in, they all told him that they had each tried to get their family members in. *"They're not letting anybody in,"* they told him.

As Rock was standing there talking to the men, the commander-in-chief pulls up in a car and walks over. He started to yell at the men, *"What are you guys doing? You didn't finish this thing yet? Is this going to be ready in two weeks?"*

Then he turned to Rock, *"What are you doing out of uniform?"* Rock was too frightened to even respond, so one of the men spoke up and said that Rock was a carpenter and was giving them some tips on how to build the office. He explained that Harvey had brought him to try to get him into the company. The commander asked Rocco if he could build him his office in two weeks; and Rocco replied, *"I'll be here tomorrow with my tools, Sir."*

He said, *"Go upstairs and tell the Captain to sign you in tonight and give you a letter for the draft board."*

So Rock walked back up those stairs (once again praising God!). And the Captain was coming out of his office, locking the door. He told him he needed to give him a letter for the draft board, and the Captain said, *"I told you there was nothing I could do for you."*

Rock said, *"No, there's a guy in a dress uniform down there who says you need to give me this letter."* So the Captain took Rock to the balcony to show him which gentleman had said that, and right when they got to the edge and looked down the commander looked up.

"Captain, did he get his letter?"

The Captain shouted back, *"Sir, the offices are already closed!"*

The commander sternly yelled, *"Well, open them up and get him his letter because he's going to build me this office!"*

So Rock was enlisted in the National Guard and excitedly went home to tell Mom.

"Mom, you're not going to believe it! I'm in the National Guard!" He said to her. And Mom just looked at him and said in her broken English, *"I no believe it?? I tell a you, you no go?!"*

So Rock went through basic training and simply had to report to the armory once a month. He was able to stay stateside during the Vietnam War. Just like Mom had said!

In time, my other brother Frank was drafted. Rock wanted to speak with the Colonel about it and see if anything would be done; but he never seemed to have an opportunity to speak with him. Mom brought the situation before the Lord in prayer, and believed that He would make a way. The next week, Rock was chosen to drive the Colonel on a four-hour road trip: that was his opportunity! He shared with him about Frank's draft, and he happened to mention that Frank was a pilot. The Colonel said there was an opening in the National Guard's helicopter school, and he could try to get him in.

Sure enough, Frank graduated from helicopter school as a Captain; and he, too, was spared from going to Vietnam. Because of his helicopter training, Frank's career in aviation climbed to another dimension. He became a well-known corporate pilot; and even flew for Warner Brothers; flying many famous and prominent people around the world.

The Lord always responded to Mom's prayers of faith. *"I tell you the truth, my Father will give you anything you ask for in My Name... Ask and you will receive, so that your joy will be complete."* (John 16:23-24)

Chapter Nine

BIRTH OF THE BANANA CART

∞

While we were growing up, Dad worked at the Brooklyn Navy Yard as a machinist. It was the top job at the time, and his salary was excellent. Dad was a faithful worker and was well-liked at his job, both by his co-workers and supervisors. However, in 1950 the Navy Yard shut down and Dad was transferred to the Navy Yard in New Jersey. The real test of faith came when Dad got completely laid off a few months later. Jobs were scarce, and all the work Dad could find was small odds and ends jobs. His salary was reduced to $39 a week; yet Mom did not panic. She had learned through her faith in God that Dad's job was not her source: God was. So she put her faith to the test in a mighty way during this time of great need.

Prayer birthed in Mom an idea. She decided she would sell fruit to support the family. She contacted Zi Peppe (Uncle Joe) who was in the fruit business in the city. Mom asked him to get us a pushcart (what you would sell fruit in); but he said that pushcarts were hard to come by. They were a rare commodity because they were not being made anymore. He went down to the Lower East Side to look for a pushcart, but there was none to be found. He came back and told Mom that there were none and that it would be almost impossible to get one. Mom insisted that God had told her there would be one there. To appease Mom, Zi Peppe went back and looked again: and sure enough, there was a pushcart there! It had just been returned because it was missing its front wheel. He arranged for Mom and Dad to purchase the pushcart for only $20! Mom's prayers were being answered; and her fruit business had officially begun.

Mom contacted a man who could supply her with bananas. He came and stocked Mom's pushcart with a few hundred pounds of bananas; and it was so overloaded, that Mom needed the man to help her wheel the cart down to the corner. She set up her banana cart on the corner of Ralph Avenue and Monroe Street. Mom told the gentleman that she would want the same amount of bananas the next day, and that she would pay him then for this first load. When the man came the next morning with the next load of fruit, he was really surprised that Mom had sold all the bananas from the day before. The corner she was selling at was not a very busy intersection, and he was amazed that she had been able to sell all the fruit. Mom said to him, *"The Lord is the one who has prospered me. This is His business, and He knows what He is doing."* Mom paid him for the bananas from the day before, and for the new ones as well. She was already debt free, and on her way to building her prosperous business.

Mom was blessed because she was delighting in the Lord. *"Blessed is the man who does not walk in the counsel of the wicked or stand in the way of sinners or sit in the seat of mockers. But his delight is in the law of the Lord, and on His law he meditates day and night. He is like a tree planted by streams of water, which yields it fruit in season and whose leaf does not wither. Whatever he does prospers."* (Psalm 1:1-3)

Chapter Ten

"YOU'LL GO CRAZY PRAYING LIKE THAT!"

∽

Mom faithfully prayed for twenty minutes three times everyday (morning, afternoon, and evening). She would kneel on the floor in her bedroom in such a way that her legs blocked the door. I remember all of us children getting ready for school every morning, needing Mom for one reason or another, and not being able to open her bedroom door. Mom would ignore our whining and complaining until her prayer time was over. *Then* we could talk with her.

Mom never let anything interrupt her time with God. Dad, in an almost humorous way, would always say, *"Katie! You'll go crazy praying like that!"* But Mom knew her contact with God was essential. She believed in putting firsts things first; and she knew her spiritual condition was more important than anything else. That did not change when she started selling fruit.

One day I came home from school a little earlier that usual. When I went to meet Mom at the pushcart, she was not there. No one was attending the pushcart! I did not know where she could have been, so I waited there for her. Finally, she came back.

"Where were you? What happened that you would leave the bananas unattended?!"

Mom replied, *"I was doing what I always do at this time: praying!"*

"You just leave the pushcart? What if someone steals the bananas?"

"Do you think it's the bananas that meets our needs? No! It's the Lord that has provided what we have. If someone takes something off the pushcart, let him have it. I'm not going to let anything distract me from my time with the Lord."

As a result of her prayers, the Lord blessed Mom's business dealings. He gave her favor with all men. Someone asked mom if she wanted to set up a fruit stand in front of his grocery store, which was located on a very busy intersection. So we "moved up" from a pushcart to a fruit stand; and we did so in time for us to store the fruit in the store's cellar during the cold weather. Because of the extra space, we could both store and sell more fruit. When the weather got colder, Mom could stand inside the store and still watch her stand. While she was inside, she learned more about dealing with customers and being a business woman by watching the store owner. God had set the whole thing up; and the Lord continued to bless her as, step by step, He prepared her path.

After a few more months, Mom was approached by a man who owned a butcher shop on Ralph Avenue. He had shut the store to take a leave of absence for health reasons and asked if she would take half the store and split the rent with him. Mom sought guidance from her pastor, and he said she should take it. So Mom went for it.

The butcher never returned. The Lord in His excellent timing made a way for us to be totally indoors by winter. We were on the increase as we "moved up" again—from the push cart, to the fruit stand, to a store of our own! We had full use of scales, butcher blocks, showcases, walk-in refrigeration, and slicing machines. Mom eventually started selling pasta, tomato sauce, and soon switched to a full line of groceries.

One night, while Mom was praying, she sensed that something was wrong over at the store, so she walked over. Dad was standing at the register with two men, and it appeared as though he was simply ringing them up. Mom stood outside the door, and watched. When one of them noticed mom, he nudged his buddy abruptly, they both left. They had been getting ready to rob the store when Mom showed up! God once again proved His faithfulness.

The Lord always showed Himself strong through Mom's prayers. Her faithful prayers brought prosperity and provision to our family. *"The prayer of a righteous man is powerful and effective."* (James 5:16b)

Chapter Eleven

BUSHELS AND BUSHELS OF PEACHES

Mom developed into a wise, resourceful business woman who could sell absolutely anything. One day Mom and I went to the marketplace to buy fruit for our store. However, when we arrived, all the stands were closed because it was a Jewish holiday. *"Let's go home, Mom. They're all closed!"*

"No, God told me to come to the marketplace today. So I am staying. We are going to buy some fruit."

"But Mom! Everyone is closed!! Let's go!" Mom could not be persuaded. She heard from the Lord and would not be talked out of it. So I left her there, and took a bus home. A little while later I heard a loud truck coming up the street. I ran outside for a better look and ...Was that Mom in the Cab?! As the truck pulled up right in front of me I saw that it

was Mom! She climbed out of the cab and I asked her what this was. She said that she had bought peaches. I asked her how many and for how much.

"Oh, I got a deal because I bought the whole truckload." The truck driver began to unload the peaches—thirty-five huge bushels of big, ripe peaches.

"But, Mom! We'll never be able to sell all these," I protested, knowing I would end up carting them to the dump. *"They too ripe!"*

Mom put me to work opening up the bushels. Before I had even finished, people were lined up to buy some. By the end of the day, every single peach had been sold! While we were closing up shop, I looked around to find one last, straggling peach for me to eat—but there were none to be found! How we had sold thirty-five bushels of peaches in one day, I had no idea; but every peach was gone!

"I am still confident of this: I will see the goodness of the Lord in the land of the living." (Psalm 27:13) Mom believed that she would see the "goodness of the Lord" in her life and in the lives of her family; and as a result, we

saw God's goodness manifested in our lives. Deuteronomy 28:5 says, *"Blessed shall be your basket and your store;"* and we were living testimonies of that.

Chapter Twelve

OUR STORE: THE STOREHOUSE

∞

Mom and Dad were both givers by nature, and they truly cared for the needs of their children more than they cared about making money in the store. They were never slow to give nor quick to hold back.

I will never forget the big sheet of cheesecake that we would sell by the slice. Dad would always let us kids take as much of it as we wanted before he sold the rest. I remember one time a woman came in to the store and saw me and my brothers and sisters taking and eating some cheesecake. She got so mad! She said she was going to tell Dad what we were doing and that we were eating all his profits. She came back and, sure enough, spoke her mind to Dad. She was furious!

"I always come in here to buy cheesecake, and there is never enough left for me to buy a decent amount of it. Your kids sit behind the

counter and eat it! They are eating up all your profits!"

Dad looked at her long and hard before he spoke. *"Listen, lady. The cheesecake is for the kids. Everything in the store is for the kids. It is all for them first, and whatever is left, we sell. If you want a bigger piece of cheesecake, you better come by early."*

That story became something that we would laugh and joke about; but it showed us that we always came first. We always knew that our parents loved and cared for us, and we had the assurance that they would always be there for us.

As we prospered in the business that God had given to us, money became a tool for evangelism. *"You will be made rich in every way so that you can be generous on every occasion."* (II Corinthians 9:11) Mom literally had bags of money strewn throughout the house. Any closet you looked in, you were bound to find a few bags of money. Because of our prosperity, we were able to be a blessing to others. Many people who used to criticize Mom and say she was "crazy" for doing the things we had done, ended up coming to her for help. Many family members in need also came to Mom, and moved with compassion, Mom always gave freely. I remember one time, a close relative came to Mom crying that the shylarks were after him. He owed money to the mafia, and if he didn't pay it, they would harm him and his family. He had no money with which to pay off his debt, so he came to Mom for help. Mom went to the closet, and pulled out a bag of money to give to him. Mom knew that it was a blessing to give; and she chose to be a giver.

"Remember the words of the Lord Jesus, how He said, 'It is more blessed to give than to receive'." (Act 20:35)

Chapter Thirteen

REAPING THE HARVEST

In 1952, our family became complete with the addition of Kathy, the seventh child. Two years later, Mom and Dad decided we needed to move out of Bushwick. It was time for a change and a nicer neighborhood for all of us to grow up in. As usual, Mom scouted around until she found just the right house, on 61st Street in Glendale, Queens. It was a brick house in a nice neighborhood. The area was very refined and quiet—completely the opposite of where we had been living in Brooklyn. In another big move, again she called out to Dad, *"Come on, Tony! It's time to move on!"*

We sold our house for $6,000, and Mom bargained the owners of the new house down to $13,500. We put $7,000 down; over half the price of the house! The house had two apartments, three garages, and a store beneath it. We were on the increase!

Mom and Dad immediately had the store renovated; and by the time we were through with it, we had a state-of-the-art. "Italian— American Superette", fully stocked with top-of-the-line equipment. Mom's vision to make the store the ultimate in its time came to pass. It was one of the most modern grocery stores in its day; and the business continued to flourish and grow.

We viewed the store as a testimonial of God's faithfulness to us. He had taken care of us from the pushcart to the superette! He had never left us high and dry; and He had never left us down and out. His hand had always been upon us, guiding us and ordering our steps.

In Mark 4:26-29, Jesus describes the Kingdom of God: "He also said, *'This is what the Kingdom of God is like. A man scatters seed on the ground. Night and day, whether he sleeps or gets up, the seed sprouts and grows, though he does not know how. All by itself the soil produces grain—first the stake, then the head, then the full kernel in the head. As soon as the grain is ripe, he puts the sickle to it, because the harvest has come'.*" The Kingdom of God, this parable teaches us is progressive.

At times the progress may seem slow or even unnoticeable; but, as Jesus said, eventually there is a great harvest from a tiny seed planted. And Mom had sown countless seeds! We were reaping the harvest of her seeds of prayer and sacrificial giving... And the harvest was abundant!

Chapter Fourteen

THE GROWTH OF THE FAMILY

∞

We found that the real reason God had brought us to Queens was for us to meet our lifelong mates. My sister Angie met her husband Augie; Frank met Maureen; Rocco met Lynn; Donna met Anthony; and Anthony met his wife Marie. I met my wife Janet in the summer of 1956. One day she walked into the store and ordered a liverwurst sandwich with ketchup. As I fixed it for her I thought, *"She sure is cute; but what a strange combination!"* We were married in the winter of 1957.

Because of the Lord showing Mom and Dad the right place to move and their willingness to listen to Him, God was able to bless us with the mates He knew should be with us the rest of our lives.

In 1970, Donna and her husband Anthony moved to Holbrook, Long Island—first of our family to move out of the city. Soon, Frank and Maureen, Angie and Augie, and Janet and I followed suit. Janet and I moved out to Lake Ronkonkoma and Angie moved near Donna in Holbrook. Rock was considering buying a house in Holbrook, ten miles off exit 57 on the Long Island Expressway. Mom liked the house and said that if only it was near her daughters, she would want to buy it.

"Let's see how far it is," Rock said. Unfamiliar with how to get around on Long Island and not sure how to get to Donna's on the back roads, they drove ten miles back to the Expressway and drove four more exits to Donna's house. When they got there and explained to her what they were doing and about the house they had been looking at, Donna said, *"That sounds like the new houses being built around the corner. Why don't we take a look at those?"* They got in the car, and Donna led them around the block to see the new development of houses. There was the house they had been looking at—right around the block! They had driven in a huge circle, because of their unfamiliarity with the roads, and ended up right back where they had started!

My parents bought the house and moved in during the spring of 1973. Mom had been praying that she would be close to her children; and the Lord gave her the desire of her heart. He was directing her steps...even with a little added humor!

Chapter Fifteen

"WHO ARE THE DOCTORS?"

∽

In 1974, when Rock and Lynn's first child Jennifer was about six month old, she began to have seizures. Jennifer's pediatrician told Lynn to bring her to a neurosurgeon at New York City University Hospital. After many tests, the doctors diagnosed Jennifer's condition as encephalitis. They kept her in the hospital, and she grew progressively worse. She shriveled up like a vegetable, and she began to have up to fifty seizures a day. About a month after she had been admitted, I went and visited Jennifer at the hospital. She looked so bad, that when I came back from the hospital, I said to Mom, *"We probably won't see Jennifer again."*

The next morning, the neurosurgeon told Rock and Lynn that, given Jennifer's present condition and weakened state, she probably would not live more that two or three days. When Rock heard that, it was like the fluorescent light in the room went out. The room filled with gloom and despair, and Rock felt like all hope was gone. He and Lynn were devastated.

Later that afternoon, Mom came to the hospital. Rock and Lynn were sitting beside Jennifer in the hospital room when Mom walked in. *"What's the matter here? Why you look like that? <u>Fesso</u>!"* She blurted out when she saw them "<u>Fesso</u>" is a Italian phrase that basically means "You're <u>dumb</u>! You're being fooled!" Mom could see that Rock and Lynn were foolishly allowing the devil to take advantage of them, and she told them so.

Rock and Lynn were taken back. I am sure they were hoping for some consolation and comfort from Mom, and she comes in calling them dumb fools?! Mom was angry! She did not understand how they could sit there looking so hopeless, having already forgotten about all the other miracles that God had done! She knew that if they had been <u>mindful</u> of all that God had already done and the ways He had proven His faithfulness, then they would not have been sitting there so depressed.

Rock said, *"Mom! The neurosurgeon said*

Mom gathers the family before she went to
be with the Lord

Mom and Dad at our first Tent Meeting

Tent Meeting

69

My wife Janet and our four children:
David, Deanine, Denise and Daniel

Mom and I preaching together

Mom's seven children

Special time with Mom

Mom with Jennifer (who received the miraculous healing) Jeanne and Deanine in 1979

Mom speaking to the church

Mom and Dad with our children on Easter Sunday

Mom, Dad, Donna, Angie, Rocco and myself

*My sister Angie giving her testimony on how God healed her eyes in
the old church (formerly the nightclub on Portion Road)*

Mom preaching at the Tent Meeting with Dad and her sons

Mom and Dad on their 50th Wedding Anniversary

Mom watching and praying for the family

that Jennifer only has two or three days to live."

"Who? Who tell you that?"

Rock said to her, *"The doctor, Mom. The 'big doctor'."*

She said to him, *"I've got a bigger Doctor than this!"*

"But Mom, the doctor said she has only two or three days. Look at her!"

Mom said she didn't want to look. Then she said, *"You go downstairs and eat a nice dinner. Everything be all right!"*

The Holy Spirit was all over Mom; and when she said that, the Holy Spirit filled the room with faith and hope. It was as if the lights came back on. They had gone off when the doctor spoke, and they went back on when Mom spoke words of faith and life! Rock and Lynn immediately went down and got something to eat.

That night around 11:00, their family doctor called. He said, *"I know the neurosurgeon gave you a horrible report: but we have one thing left to try. We want to put Jennifer on cortisone. It's a dangerous drug for a baby so small; but we've only got a few days left, and we've got to try something."* So they gave Jennifer a shot of cortisone.

That night, as she had every night for the past month, Lynn stayed with Jennifer. And she watched in amazement as she saw Jennifer's hair, which had been perfectly straight for six months, begin to curl. It looked like she got a perm! And Lynn sat there amazed as Jennifer slept through the night without having one seizure! She had been having seizures every half hour or so—and she didn't have one that night!

The next morning, Jennifer began to cry— which she had not done at all the whole month she was in the hospital. The neurosurgeon walked in, looked at Jennifer and said, *"What did you do to her? She looks different!"* He looked over her chart and was shocked. *"No seizures?! Are you sure?!"*

Lynn was crying and she said, *"No, doctor, she had no seizures. And she cried for the first time this morning. Doctor, Jennifer received a miracle last night."*

The doctor took the baby and ran some tests on her. He came back a little while later and said, *"Remember the test we had done which said that Jennifer was 99% abnormal? Now the test is showing that she is perfect! We gave her one cortisone shot last night—it couldn't have been that. That medicine doesn't work that way. It would take months and months of receiving those shots to produce results. You know what happened here last night? This is a miracle from God!"*

A total miracle had occurred! After a few days of follow-up tests, Jennifer was released from the hospital, a happy, healthy baby! Because Mom had looked through the eyes of faith and spoke words of life over the situation, the Lord was able to work nightly. Rock and Lynn had their daughter back.

Chapter Sixteen

LIFE MORE ABUNDANTLY

∽

Because our family was blessed, the enemy was always there trying to rob from us. John 10:10 tells us that *"the devil comes not but for to steal, and to kill, and to destroy; but I (Jesus) have come that you might have life, and life more abundantly."*

Shortly after Angie and Augie first moved to Holbrook in 1972, Angie began to experience eye trouble. Her vision became blurry and unclear. The doctor said it was related to her pregnancy (she was pregnant with her third child), and that she needed to learn to live with it. However, within a few months her eyes began to give out without warning. She could hardly do a thing around the house since she never knew when it would happen. Light aggravated the problem, so Angie kept the house dark. Oppression settled over her; and, terrified she would go completely blind, she lived in a continual state of torment.

After several years of dealing with this horrible situation, Angie happened to turn on *The 700 Club*, a Christian television program. Pat Robertson, the show's host, encouraged her by preaching Jesus Christ as the Almighty Healer. He gave her new hope. Then he gave an opportunity for those who needed a relationship with Jesus to accept Him as Lord. Angie felt deeply convicted and fell to her knees. She prayed right there in front of the television screen, confessing Jesus as Lord and giving Him control of her life. She called me to tell me she had given her life to Jesus and that she believed God would take care of her. She sounded so much better; I knew something was going to happen.

During this time, God had given Angie two dreams. The first dream occurred before her conversion. In her dream Jesus was standing beside her bed, with tears rolling down His face. His eyes were filled with compassion, but He did not speak. She understood that the tears were for her. Later the Lord showed her through His Word that His *"people are destroyed from lack of knowledge"* (Hosea 4:6). God was showing her that although He desired to heal her, He could not do so unless she turned to Him.

Shortly after her confession of faith in Jesus, she had the second dream. She dreamed that she was in a large auditorium, filled with people. An evangelist was preaching and he walked over to her. When he was right in front of her, he turned into a statue; and Jesus appeared behind him. He reached out His hands and, with eyes full of compassion, touched her. In the dream, she was completely healed. This gave Angie new hope.

Not long after this, Dad saw an evangelist on TV who would pray for people, and he sometimes saw miracles taking place right on the screen. The evangelist announced a meeting he was holding at the Brooklyn Academy of Music in January, 1976. We decided to go; and the Lord gave Angie the strength and courage to believe for her healing.

On January 18th, the family piled into Dad's station wagon for the 60-mile drive to Brooklyn. It was hard for Angie to sit in a car for more that a few minutes without getting carsick, and she had to wear thick, dark glasses to keep the light from her eyes; but she had God's assurance throughout the trip. I had to work that day and could not join the rest of the family; but I promised the Lord that if He would heal Angie I would give my life fully to Him.

They arrived at the meeting and sat in the middle of the auditorium. The evangelist preached on healing. Then he walked over and laid his hands on Angie. Suddenly she stood up and screamed, *"I can see!"* Her eye sight was fully restored!

When I arrived home late from work that afternoon, Janet came running to the car and told me what had happened. Later that evening, I knelt down and thanked God for Angie's healing. I committed my life to Him and told Him, *"I'm Yours, Lord."*

Chapter Seventeen

FAMILY PRAYER MEETINGS

Angie's healing caused the family to turn more towards the Lord. Janet and I purchased a Bible, which we took turns reading. One day, I read: *"But seek first His kingdom and His righteousness, and all these things will be given you as well."* (Matthew 6:33) The words seemed to jump off the page at me. For the first time in my life, I was seeing the written Word of God as applying directly to me. I had never seen with such clarity the depth and the truth of the Scriptures as I did that day. My life was turning around; and, in the ensuing days, the Lord started to open up the Scriptures to me so that I could understand His Word. Janet and I continued to read the Bible; and as we sought Him on a daily basis, the Lord began to reveal more and more of His perfect will to us.

In September of 1976, the same evangelist

held another crusade in New York City. Janet and I attended with some other family members. Someone who worked in the ministry of this evangelist recognized Kathy from videos of Angie's healing and after we talked with him, we invited him to come over to the house for the holidays. When he came to Mom and Dad's house, he encouraged us to come together once a week to pray as a whole family. So we began to meet on Friday nights in Mom's kitchen; and soon our friends and neighbors joined us.

One day Kathy went to a meeting at a Spirit-filled fellowship. When she walked into our next Friday night meeting, her face was glowing. As she spoke, she seemed more expressive and bolder than usual. She explained to us about the baptism of the Holy Spirit and her new heavenly language. Then she beckoned for me to stand up and receive it. I was hungry for it; but I felt unworthy. I also wanted Janet to receive it with me, but Janet was not there; so I stayed in my seat and said I preferred to wait until next week. She prayed over someone else, who instantly received the infilling and began to speak in a strange, but beautiful, language. My heart was bursting. I became so excited that I said to myself, *"I can't wait."* As if she was reading my mind, Kathy said, *"God wants to give you the Holy Spirit now. You don't have to wait, Dan."* This time I could not argue.

She laid hands on me and instructed me to thank the Lord for the gift of the baptism of the Holy Spirit. All at once I started to stammer. My lips started to move and at first only a few sounds came. When I sat down, my language flowed out. I was so excited that I could not sit still.

When Dad walked in from work, he was quite surprised to see us all there praying in another tongue. He asked what was going on. I walked over to him and explained that I had been filled with the Holy Spirit. I told him I wanted to pray for him. He said, *"Well, if you want to pray for me, pray for my stomach."* I laid hands on him and prayed for healing. The burning sensation in his stomach immediately left, and Dad was totally healed.

God had so gloriously filled me that I felt His supernatural love gushing out all over me. When I walked into the house that night, Janet was asleep. I prayed over her in my new language, asking God to fill her with His Spirit.

The next day I told her what had happened, and she said, *"I want it, too."* She received the baptism of the Holy Spirit; and within several months, the whole family was speaking in tongues. *"Whoever believes in Me, as the Scripture has said, streams of living water will flow from within him."* (John 7:38)

Chapter Eighteen

The Basement Church

∞

Our fellowship continued to grow. When we could longer fit everyone into the kitchen, we moved to the den. Soon, though, there were too many people for that room as well. Rock and I ran a home improvement business at the time, so we decided to renovate Mom and Dad's basement. We painted the floor, decorated the walls and installed a bathroom. We started to meet every Friday night in the basement church. We would sit in chairs set up in a semicircle, all facing the pulpit.

After six months, the Lord spoke to Angie about holding regular Sunday services. When Angie shared that with me, I was very reluctant about making such a big transition I told her that the Lord would really have to let us know that it was of Him before we would make a decision to do that.

One Friday night shortly after that, Janet's friend Tina, a Catholic woman, came to the basement church. As we were sitting there, Tina suddenly let out a gasp. Being she was Catholic, my first thought was that we had offended her. However, when someone asked Tina what was wrong, she replied, *"I can't believe what I'm seeing!"* She pointed at the floor in the center of the circle of chairs, in front of the pulpit. *"Don't you see it? Look on the floor!"* We all stared at the floor, to the place where she was pointing, but we could not see a thing. *"It's the profile of Jesus' face! Don't you see it?"* I got up, and ran over to where Tina was sitting; and looked at the floor. At first, I did not see anything; and then...I let out a gasp! There on the floor before me, right in the center of the chairs, was the outline of Jesus' face. It was so clear.

I took that as the sign from the Lord that we were to go ahead with having Sunday services. I felt like it was His stamp of approval. As we obeyed and began to hold Sunday Services, the Lord manifested His presence in marvelous healings and deliverances. Attendance grew as God *"confirmed His Word with signs following."* (Mark 16:20)

The "face of Jesus" remained on the basement floor. I don't know exactly what it was that caused it to be there: possibly just the strokes of paint from when we had painted the floor; but it was a constant reminder of the fact that God was in on what we were doing. Many times visitors who came to the basement church would say, "Show us the sign!", and all the glory was given to the Lord! *"And these signs will accompany those who believe..."* (Mark 16:17)

Chapter Nineteen

GOD GETS A HOLD OF DAN

∞

Janet and I have four children—Daniel, Denise, David and Deanine— whose hearts are all turned toward the Lord. Daniel, however, went through a period of rebellion. Having been reared in the Catholic church, he could not understand why we were speaking in tongues and praying for miracles. As soon as he graduated high school, Dan moved out to live with a friend. He got involved with the wrong crowd; and Janet and I trusted that He was in God's hands and we knew that God would bring him around.

At Christmas time, the entire family gathered at Mom's, as we always did around the holidays. Because Dan was not living at home anymore, I was not sure if he would join the family at Mom's house; but he came with his girlfriend Stacy so that she could meet the family. After dinner, we all moved into the living room where we sat around sharing about the Lord and what He was doing in our lives.

I knew that Dan felt uncomfortable, so I was not surprised when he stood up and started to say good-bye to everybody. As he walked toward the front door, Mom called out from the corner of the room where she sat, *"Dan! Come here. I want to pray for you."* Dan insisted he and Stacy really had to go. *"Another time, Granma."* They went back and forth a few times until Dan had the front door open, ready to walk out. The rest of us in the living room sat there praying under our breath. We could sense the spiritual battle that was going on.

Mom looked at Stacy and said, *"Stacy, I want to pray for you, too. Come here."* Stacy told Dan to let Mom pray; so he finally relented. He closed the door and walked over to Mom. Mom placed her hands on Dan and Stacy and started to pray in tongues. When Mom's hands began to tremble, all of us in the room knew that the Spirit of God had shown up! Then Mom prophesied over the two of them. She said that God had a plan for their lives; that they would serve the Lord and be used by Him to bring forth the truth of the Gospel and to turn many from darkness to light. She said they would be a team, and work hand-in-hand to serve God's people; and that the Lord would give Dan tremendous boldness.

When Mom finished praying and Dan and Stacy left, the whole family started rejoicing. We knew that God had His way, and that we would soon see the results of Mom's prayers. We knew that it would only be a matter of time before Dan fully gave his life to the Lord.

One night shortly after that, Dan came home from a party at one in the morning, and, looking for something to read, he nonchalantly picked up the Bible. He began to read the Psalms out loud. The words felt like they were echoing inside him; and he was deeply convicted. He cried out to the Lord in repentance, and invited Jesus to be the Lord of his life. The next day while driving to work, his roommate Joe asked him why he was playing the drums in the middle of the night. Dan, quite surprised and confused, told him that he didn't own drums, only a guitar. Joe insisted that he heard drums coming from Dan's room the night before. He said that he had tried to get up and yell at him, but he felt pinned to the bed and could not move. Dan was perplexed about the incident, but he felt that it had something to do with conversion.

Later on the Lord showed him in the Word that *"there is rejoicing in the presence of the angels of God over one sinner who repents."* (Luke 15:10) Dan believed that his roommate had heard a physical manifestation of the angels' rejoicing.

After the Lord got hold of his life, Dan was a changed young man. His shy personality suddenly transformed into one of great boldness and confidence. All his friends noticed the change in his life and saw that he had completely turned his life around, which gave him many opportunities to minister to them. Dan even moved back home and started to come to the basement church with us. The first night he came, I asked him to share his testimony. He stood up, walked behind the pulpit, and boldly shared what God had done in his life. Everyone was in awe at how powerfully he spoke. The Lord had truly given Dan a *"spirit of power"* rather than a *"spirit of timidity"* (II Timothy 1:7); and every Friday night after that, Dan would get up and share something at the basement church fellowship.

Once again, Mom's prayers had changed the circumstances, and we saw the Word of God prove true: *"Believe in the Lord Jesus, and you will be saved—you and your household."* (Acts 16:31)

Chapter Twenty

DAD'S TRANSFORMATION

During our family fellowships, Dad would just watch and listen. He did not really participate in what we were doing. He never seemed to need any help. Dad did not think that he "needed" God like Mom did, and he could never understand her praying all the time. He constantly nagged Mom about it, telling her that, *"You'll go crazy praying like that!"*

However, one day, Mom heard some noise coming from the basement. She opened the door quietly and saw Dad crying on his knees. She called down and asked him, *"What are you doing down there?"*

"Katie, I'm praying in the Spirit...and I can't stop crying!" A smile formed on her face and she chuckled as she called down to him, *"Tony! You'll go crazy praying like that!"*

Because of Mom's prayers for him all those years, Dad had found God; and he was a changed man as a result! Mom's prayers for him brought about such a transformation in his life, that even certain things about his character changed. *"Therefore, if anyone is in Christ, he is a new creation; the old has gone, the new has come!"* (II Corinthians 5:17) Years before, when Donna and Angie were in their twenties, Dad came home from work and told them that he had bought them each a small flashlight for their key rings. The girls complained, *"But Daddy, why do we need flashlights on our keychains? Flashlights are for boys. Give them to them!"*

Dad insisted that they put the flashlights on their keychains. *"I was walking on Ludlow Street and something came over me telling me to get you girls a flashlight. I think it was God that made me do this, so put them on your keyrings!"*

When the girls began to whine about it again, Dad said, *"God told me to get this for you. I know it!"* Reluctantly the girls agreed and put the flashlights on their keyrings.

They would have said, *"Okay,"* and not

made a big deal about it. But they felt that he had heard the voice of the Lord, because he was very insistent about the flashlights.

The next evening around 5:30, Angie and Donna were in the subway together, coming home from work in Manhattan. They stepped into the train, and the doors closed. All of a sudden the doors opened again, and Angie turned to Donna and said she felt like they should get off. So they turned and stepped off the train, and just as they stepped onto the platform, all of the lights went out in the subway—and it was pitch black in the subway! Suddenly Angie and Donna remembered that they had flashlights in their pocketbooks. They pulled them out, turned them on, and began to find their way out of the subway. People started to shout, *"Look! There's a light! Let's follow it!"*, and the whole crowd of thousands of people followed Donna and Angie safely out of the subway!

Mom's prayers went much further than herself. They affected Dad and each one of us children. They even affected the New York subway system that day in 1965!

Chapter Twenty-one

THE LORD WORKS ALL THINGS FOR GOOD

∞

On quite a few occasions, the devil really tried to destroy Mom and Dad. In the winter of 1960, my sister Donna had just arrived at her office in New York City when she received a telephone call. A friend of the family was on the line, telling her that the "Constellation", the aircraft carrier Dad worked on at the Brooklyn Navy Yard, was in flames and hundreds of people were trapped. Donna screamed, dropped the telephone, and ran outside into the snow. She was crying and praying for God to spare her father and the other people on the burning ship.

She walked block after block, tears streaming down her face, trying to find a taxicab to take her home; but she finally gave up and headed for the subway. During the hour-and-fifteen-minute subway ride, Donna continued to cry to God. *"Please, Heavenly*

Father, in Jesus Name, save my Dad! He is so very much needed—the father of seven children, the youngest being only six years old!"

After arriving in Queens, Donna had to catch a bus, then walk a few blocks before coming to her street. As she approached the house, she saw the family car with its hood open and a man with his head under the hood. She had a pit in her stomach and she called out, *"Dad! Dad! Is it you?"* Just as she was about to faint, the man looked up and Donna realized that it was Dad! He ran over to her, held her in his arms, and reassured her that he was fine. He said, *"What are you worried about, Donna? Didn't you know that Mom would have been praying? She called the whole family into agreement."*

Mom had known that God would be faithful. She had the assurance that after she and the family had prayed, God would intervene and Dad would be safe—which he was. Later we found out what had happened. Because of the type work he was doing that morning on the ship, Dad was required to wear earphones. Through the earphones, he heard distress signals and knew that everyone was to abandon the ship. Dad ran to all the co-workers, warning them of the grave situation. Fifty people died, but Dad was able to get off the ship in time, along with many co-workers who followed him to safety.

Another time, during a Sunday morning church service in 1985, Dad fell out of his chair, and lay motionless on the ground. Mom jumped up and gasped, *"Jesus!"* I walked over to Dad and commanded the spirit of death to leave his body. Instantly, he came back to life. We carried him into my office, and Mom took him home. After the service, Janet and I went over to their house to see him. We expected Dad to be in bed, being cared for, however, when we arrived, he met us at the door! *"I'm glad you're here. I'm cooking for Mom."* He looked and felt fine. The Lord had miraculously intervened in his life!

A few months later, I awoke in the middle of the night from a dream in which I saw two coffins. I did not know who they belonged to, but I began to intercede. I bound the spirit of death and prayed in the Spirit. The following day, Mom and Dad were in their way home from the store, when their car was broadsided by another car. The accident was horrendous and they both should have been killed, but

Dad walked away without a scratch. Mom's neck had cracked. She stayed in the hospital for three weeks, where she wore a steel halo attached with screws to her skull (to keep her neck from moving). When she was sent home, nurses came every day to care for her. During her long recovery at home, she went through about twelve nurses. By the time she was fully recovered, each of the nurses had gotten saved, and over half had received the baptism of the Holy Spirit! They knew that Mom should not have walked away from the accident alive; and they saw God in His faithfulness perfectly heal her body.

What the devil had meant for evil in that situation, God had turned around for good! *"And we know that in all things God works for the good of those who love Him, who have been called according to His purpose."* (Romans 8:28)

Chapter Twenty-two

THE LORD SPEAKS
THROUGH MOM

∞

My sister Kathy began to grow discouraged. She was serving the Lord wholeheartedly, and had stopped "hanging out" with her old friends. She desired to get married, but still hadn't met the "right one"; and she felt that she was never going to have an opportunity since she did not go out as much as she used to. Mom ministered to her and encouraged her by saying, *"God knows what you have need of, Kathy. You don't need to go out looking for a man. God will bring somebody to you."* Kathy relied on what Mom had said, and trusted the Lord to bring her a mate.

Meanwhile, Gene Pontillo was being ministered to by his mailman, who was a Christian. Every time the mailman had the chance to, he would share with Gene about the Lord; and Gene listened with an open heart.

The mailman gave Gene a copy of Hal Lindsay's book, <u>The Late Great Planet Earth</u> and Gene read it. The Lord touched his heart, and Gene prayed the prayer of salvation at the end of the book. He felt that his life was changed, and wanted to know more about the decision he had made, and what God had done inside him. Gene soaked it up like a sponge.

Daniel invited Gene to come to Wednesday night Bible study, where he received the baptism of the Holy Spirit. Dan then invited him to come to the basement church on Friday night. When Gene came that Friday, he met Kathy for the first time. As soon as he laid eyes on her, something jumped in his spirit and he knew that she would be his wife. She felt the same way when she saw him. They married a year later.

The Lord used Mom to speak works of faith and life over Kathy's situation; and the Lord showed Himself faithful to His Word. Psalm 37:4 says, *"Delight yourself in the Lord, and He will give you the desires of your heart."* As Kathy continued to serve the Lord and not worry about finding "Mr. Right", the Lord blessed her by bringing this tall strong handsome, sweet man to her! If Kathy had traveled around the world, she could not have found anyone better than the man God brought right to her doorstep.

I also remember a time, many years later, that the Lord used Mom to speak words of life and faith into a situation. Mom was visiting my brother Rock's church in Queens (Jesus Revival Church), where he was the pastor. After the service, she was speaking with a couple who had been married for ten years.

"You got any children?" She asked them. They said that they would like to have children, but so far had been unable to conceive.

"You want a children?" Mom asked with her broken English.

"Yes, we want children." They answered.

Mom asked it again. *"You want a children?"* She asked three or four times and the young couple just thought that maybe she was not understanding them.

Then Mom asked them if they had prayed; they had. She also asked if they had started to prepare the babies' room. They said they had not.

"Well, do you really want children? Then go to the store, pick up some pampers, and put them in the babies' dresser. In fact, get two boxes of pampers."

The couple got very excited and built up with faith; and agreed to go home and do just what she had said. Sure enough, within a few months, the young woman conceived...and nine months after that, she brought twins into the world!

The Lord used Mom's faith to build up the faith of that young couple. Then, when they took action upon it, they saw the results of it! *"Faith without works is dead."* (James 2:20)

Chapter Twenty-three

THE GARAGE CHURCH

∞

When I had first gotten saved, I was so self-conscious I could hardly speak in front of people I did not know; but after getting baptized in the Holy Spirit, an uncharacteristic boldness fell on me along with a desire to preach. In 1978, the Lord spoke directly to me about my ministry. One Saturday afternoon while I was mowing the lawn and praying in the Spirit, the Lord spoke to my heart: *"Teach My people to trust Me and to walk by faith."* He also said He wanted me to open up my home and teach His Word. I argued with Him, saying I still needed to grow; but He impressed upon me that He would teach me directly. My excitement over the fact that God had spoken to me quickly dwindled when I thought of telling Janet. I did not think she would be too excited about having a constant flow of visitors in the house. Janet was a meticulous housekeeper. She prided herself in keeping our home truly spotless and orderly. To allow visitors in and out at practically all times of day was a lot to ask and expect. I asked the Lord to deal with her heart; and I asked for favor and wisdom in expressing myself.

"Babe," I said, as we sat at the kitchen table. *"The Lord's been showing me that He wants to use me to teach believers. And He wants us to do it here, in the house."* She smiled, and said that would be fine. It was so unlike her that it had to be God. Within a month we had opened up our home on Wednesday evenings in addition to holding our regular Friday night meetings and Sunday services at Mom's.

Later that year we visited Janet's sister Doris in California. She had arranged for me to minister at several home fellowships while we were there. Each time I shared about Angie's healing, a miracle service followed. We saw many people healed by the power of God during our time in California.

A year after returning to New York, the Lord showed me He wanted me to have meetings in my home at least three days a week. I had been renovating our garage and leveling out the floor to be equal with the rest of the house, thinking we would make an apartment out of it. Instead, we decided to use it for our church. In January of 1979, we began holding meetings in our garage church on Wednesdays, Fridays, and Sundays; but we still had no idea how much God had in mind.

Chapter Twenty-four

CLAIMING THE LAND

∽

By September of 1979, we had been in our garage church for almost a year. The fellowship, which we called "Faith of God's Word Ministry", was growing and the Lord began speaking to me about having our own building. One Monday night I passed a disco/bar named "Faces" as I was driving down Portion Road in the town of Farmingville. I marveled at how many cars filled the parking lot, even on a Monday night. Then the Lord impressed upon me that the building would soon be used for God's glory and that people would come from all over to fill it.

While passing "Faces" again on my way home, I heard the Lord's voice a second time. He told me to go to the disco and bind the works of the devil. So I pulled into the parking lot and laid my hands on the building, cursing the Posers of darkness, and commanding the devil to release his hold.

The following Saturday morning, Janet and I returned with our youngest daughter Deanine. We walked around the building, as the Israelites had done around the walls of Jericho, and claimed it for the Lord. Then we knelt in the parking lot to thank the Lord in faith that the building was for God's people. We knew God had a sensitive ear to our prayer and that He would move heaven and earth to get us in there.

A week later I called the owners to see if they were interested in selling. They named a price of $500,000. We sent them a letter telling them that the building was going to become a church. We wrote that it would be a building that people would use everyday of the week: a place where people would be healed, the captives would be set free, the blind would receive their sight, and the bruised would receive liberty. I felt I had to make that proclamation. It was important to show it to them in writing, even if they did not understand.

Shortly afterwards, we shared with the congregation what God had shown us about the building. They began to get excited. Everyone caught the vision and was believing God for the building.

One day a local minister was driving home our daughter Deanine (five years old at the time). As they passed the building, Deanine pointed to it and said that it was our church building. He said, "No, Deanine. That's a bar. It's a disco." Again, she told him that was our church and that she would be running the bookstore. She was speaking by faith— according to what she was believing for, rather that what she was seeing.

In 1980, I called the owner to check on the status of the building and he invited me to come down to look. One of the members of our congregation had a dream about the interior of the building and said that one of the walls was a coral color. When I walked into the building, I got so excited because I saw exactly that! As the owner escorted me through the building, now undergoing renovation, I marveled at the new bathrooms, carpeting, offices and electric.

In March of 1982, I felt impressed to resign from my job as building inspector; and, shortly afterwards, the disco abruptly closed. It had appeared to be as prosperous as ever, so we were surprised by its closing; and we knew it was time for our breakthrough!

Chapter Twenty-five

POSSESSING THE LAND

In the ensuing months, my brother Frank and I negotiated with the owner, who eventually came down to $250,000. That was as far as he would go. One Sunday he let me bring Janet and the kids to see the inside of the building. We stood near the dance floor, joined hands, and prayed. Within a month he called to say he would come down to $190,000; he had seen us praying and it had touched him. He also mentioned that two other people had made higher offers but he would give it to me if I could pay the whole thing in cash.

I asked him to wait a few weeks. I was on my way to a Kenneth Copeland conference in Atlanta. As a seed of faith, I planted all the money our ministry had at that time into Kenneth Copeland's ministry—$2,000. The week we were scheduled to go to contract, a total of $10,000 was given by Frank Pilliteri, Bob and Bella Sulzer, and Tom and Kathleen

Caiati. Because of their obedience to the Lord, we had money to bring to the meeting to put down on the house.

The morning we went into contract, June 23rd, I woke up with all kinds of doubts and fears running around my head. The day finally came! We were going into contract on our building! I was nervous and apprehensive, though, because I knew that we were dealing with rough people, and that things would not be easy. I thought of what Mom would do in my situation. Mom would pray. So I knelt down by my bed and asked the Lord to give me His peace. I said, *"Lord, if the owner hands over the key of the building to me today at contract, rather than waiting until we go to closing, I will know that we can make it."* I knew that the owner giving me the key would be a sign from the Lord. As I left the house, I thanked the Lord that what I prayed for would come to pass.

At the meeting, the owner asked me if I had the money. I said that I had $10,000, but that God would meet the rest of the need. He stood up and shouted, *"Do you have the money or don't you? What do you think—that God will just drop the money from the sky! Stop playing games with me! Do you have the money or not?!"* Again I said that God would take care of it. My lawyer, also a Christian, agreed. They drew up a contract, and said I had a week to come up with the remaining ten percent, $9,000, and a month to come up with another $101,000.

I had signed all the papers, we had discussed everything, and we were getting ready to walk out when the owner called out, *"Wait, Preacher! Here's the key to your building. I don't need them anymore."* And he handed me the key. The Lord was faithful to me, and I was strengthened and encouraged that everything was going to work out.

When I got home that afternoon and showed Janet the key, she told me that she and the other women at the Woman's Meeting had been praying for me. They prayed that the owner would give me the key as a sign from the Lord. The Lord heard their prayers of faith and He answered.

That Wednesday night I dangled the key before my congregation. They were so excited that the next night many of them were over at the building cleaning up. The following Sunday we had our first service in the building. We had not yet taken down the bar, so we had church on the dance floor next to it! There we were, having church in one of the most well-known night clubs on Long Island! We were possessing the land!

Mom would always say in Italian, *"When you pray, you win,"* and she was right.

Chapter Twenty-six

INHERITING WHAT WAS PROMISED

∞

The building was perfect for us. It had two offices, a waiting area, a conference room, a tape room, and a bar and dance floor which we used for sanctuary. What joy we had in taking down the bar sign and putting up our "Faith of God's Word Ministry" sign!

July 23rd was the next meeting with the owner, and I was supposed to have $101,000 to give the owners. I had no money. They were up in arms, and they began to yell and curse. They really showed their true colors and they got very violent. It seemed as though they might seriously hurt us. And my lawyer was so frightened that he slid off his chair and ducked under the table! I told them I needed to have a talk with my lawyer, so I pulled him out from under the table, and we walked into the outside office.

"What are you so frightened about?" I asked him. *"Aren't you believing with me? I told you from the very beginning that we needed to purchase this place by faith first and that it wasn't going to be an easy road. You agreed to stand in faith with us."*

I prayed with him for the Lord to calm his fears; and we walked back into the meeting. Everything had calmed down. The Holy Spirit, with His peace, had flooded the room; and the men, who just before had seemed as though they might harm us, were now calmly asking us when we thought we could have the money. We worked out a plan to pay the balance in monthly installments until it was paid off.

Every month, the owners would come in and harass us for more money. The property was shared by a few people, and they couldn't agree on splitting the money; so they could each come in individually and harass me to give them more. They were always very rude, crude, and nasty. I spoke to Mom about what they were doing, and she replied, *"Just let them know that this is the Lord's doing and if they give you trouble, they will have trouble from God."*

The next time two of them came in, they were very upset. They were very loud and obnoxious; but I simply told them what Mom had told me to say. *"This is the Lord's doing. If you want to give me trouble, then you are going to receive trouble from God. What God has ordained, you can't change. I've prayed and the Lord will provide."*

The two of them walked out and started fist-fighting out in the parking lot! The Lord used Mom to give me wisdom on how to deal with the owners, and He turned them against themselves! *"The Lord will grant that the enemies who rise up against you will be defeated before you. They will come at you from one direction but flee from you in seven."* (Deuteronomy 28:7)

A long-time friend, Dom Giovanniello, took a look at our contract. He was concerned because a new contract had not been drawn up after we had worked out the arrangement to pay monthly. So he had the lawyers draw up a new contract, stating he would give an immediate payment of $35,000, which we eventually payed back with interest.

In the car on the way home from the

meeting, Dom turned to me and said, *"Dan, I thought you said God was going to meet the need. I met the need!"*

I told him, *"Dom, you certainly did meet the need but God uses people. He met the need through you!"*

By God's grace we paid the balance way before June—taking only seven months to pay it off, as opposed to twelve. Had we not paid the balance when we did, the deed would have been tied up in legal proceedings because the owner died a month later. The Lord was faithful, and we obtained the building! According to Hebrews 6:12, *"though faith and patience"* we inherited *"what was promised."*

Chapter Twenty-seven

FAITH ACADEMY

∞

As we became settled in the new sanctuary on Portion Road, we began to progress very quickly. In September of 1984, we opened up Faith Academy, starting with thirty-nine students. We sectioned off part of the sanctuary for classes and at night we would use it for services again.

We went through quite a battle during the beginning days of Faith Academy. When we first opened up the school, we had not known that it was necessary to have a fire inspection, a certificate of occupancy, and an underwriters certificate. The local school district gave us a certain period of time in which we needed to obtain all these things. So, we immediately obtained a fire inspection and got approvals from the architects and the electricians. However, certificates of occupancy are difficult to obtain, and there was no way we would get it in time. The superintendent of the district told us that they were going to have to close us down if we did not have it. When I shared the situation with Mom, her response was, *"If God put the vision in your heart for the school, no devil in hell can take it away from you!"* That encouraged my faith and I knew that God would show us a way out of the situation.

When the deadline came, the superintendent called me and asked if I had obtained the C.O. When I told him I had not, he said, *"You leave me no choice. As of right now, I'm getting an injunction to close down the school."* During the phone conversation, I was flipping through a handbook of legal requirements for having a school, and right then something caught my eye.

"Before you hang up," I said, *"Let me run something by you. I have in my hand the legal manual. And it says here that to have a school you need only a fire inspection or a certificate of occupancy—not both!"* The superintendent told me he needed to check into that. He said he would have to call back; and then he abruptly hung up. Ten days later he finally called.

"Pastor Cotrone, you can keep your school

open. You were right. The fire inspection was good enough by itself."

Once again the Lord had pulled through on our behalf! It was a total miracle the way the whole situation worked out; and I stood amazed at Mom's ability to see through the eyes of faith.

So Faith Academy was officially up and running! It was very small, and we used to have physical education in the hallway because we had nowhere else to do it. The kids wanted a gym and to be able to play sports. I told them that everything we had, had come through prayer, so *"Why don't we pray about it?"* We joined together, and each student asked God for a specific thing regarding the school. In time, every one of those prayers was answered! In 1986 we built a 10,000 square-foot sanctuary, seating approximately 1,200 people, We also added a new school wing and cafeteria, bringing the total capacity of our building to 33,000 square feet. The new sanctuary got put right to use for the school, not only as a chapel, but as a gymnasium as well! We started up sports programs, and our teams went on to win various league and division championships.

In 1988, we had our first graduating class. Now, ten graduating classes later, we have over 200 students. We are New York State certified and fully accredited through Oral Roberts University. Our school is on the increase, and young lives are being changed. Our students are *"taught of the Lord"* and great is their peace. (Isaiah 54:13)

Chapter Twenty-eight

THE MINISTRY EXPANDS

∞

Back in the early '80s, a local pastor had a daily fifteen-minute radio program. When I met him, he told me that he was having trouble staying on the air, because the congregation simply could not provide the funds. After consulting another pastor, the two of us decided to share the broadcast with him. We all split the air time, so I was on the air for one week each month. It was totally the Lord's doing, because He had been prompting me to go on the air; but I argued with Him, feeling unequipped. I also knew that it was very costly and I did not feel that our small congregation would be able to support it financially. I was afraid of the unknown, and I pushed off the prompting of the Lord. But as He opened up the door right before me, I knew it was completely His work.

After three months, the second pastor

resigned. Then about six months later, I was driving home from the radio station when the Lord spoke to me about taking the broadcast myself. I did not expect to hear that, but I knew it had to be God because I never would have thought of that myself. About a month later, the first pastor called. I knew why he was calling even before he said it. He could not manage the broadcast any longer, and asked if I would take it alone. In October, 1982, my radio ministry began.

I was on the radio for thirteen years, always with a message of hope and encouragement. I know, from countless testimonies, that the program truly blessed people's lives. I spoke words of faith and life over the listeners and I ended every broadcast with, *"Greater is He that is in you than he that is in the world...You fail? Impossible!"*

In 1985 we began Long Island Bible School; and in 1997 we received full accreditation through Oral Roberts University. The Bible School is still growing, as each semester we have more and more students. We are equipping this generation with the Word of God, enabling them to go out and do what the Lord is calling them to do.

As of 1994, we also have a television ministry. In the beginning of that year, I received a vision from the Lord. In my vision, I was waiting expectantly for a fishing pole. The UPS truck turned the corner onto my block. As the truck approached, it seemed to get bigger and bigger, and when it parked in front of my house I saw that it was a huge semi. I thought to myself, *"My God! What kind of a fishing pole is this?"* The whole truck opened up right before me, and there I was the biggest fishing pole I had ever seen. It was enormous! I squinted and looked the huge apparatus over, wondering to myself what kind of line it must have, being it was so large. Then I saw it—the line was a thick white cable. At that moment, I knew what the Lord was trying to tell me—we were to go on television (cable) and *"fish for souls"*.

So, in September, 1994, our half-hour long program, *Life for Today*, began. Today, it reaches over twelve million homes on Long Island and New York City, extending as far as Staten Island and Connecticut. I minister words of faith and life to the people, ending each program with *"You fail? Impossible!"*, and lives are being touched. We receive countless reports of viewers who have gotten saved via the program—even those who have been healed just by watching it! The Lord is doing miraculous things as we step out in faith, believing Him to meet all our needs. We do not solicit funds on the program, or even offer any items in exchange for a donation. We are relying solely on the Lord to keep the show running, being it was His idea in the first place.

Chapter Twenty-nine

MY CHILDREN, MY REWARD

∞

The Bible says in Psalm 127:3 that *"sons are a heritage from the Lord; children a reward from Him."* Janet and I have watched as our children have grown up to be men and women of God. They are all serving the Lord and continue to be used by Him in mighty ways.

Dan and Stacy married and helped develop our ministry in the early stages. Stacy led the music ministry, and Dan did his share of the preaching and teaching (both in Bible School and in Faith Academy). When things in our ministry settled, they went on the road with their three children (Daneille, Dominique, and Christian). They had an evangelistic ministry until 1996, when the Lord called them to begin a church in Florida. Today, Dan and Stacy are pastoring *Victory Church*, and the Lord is doing tremendous things in and through their ministry.

My daughter Denise and her husband Ed also helped out in the early days of the ministry. Ed served as the principal of Faith Academy and Bible teacher. Denise served as the school secretary and in the music ministry. They have three wonderful children, David, Amy and Jonathon.

David and his wife Dawn have two children, David and Dominic. David heads up the financial administration of our ministry and produces our television program. He and his family still play an active role here at the ministry, and it is a blessing to be able to work alongside my son.

My youngest daughter Deanine, now twenty-two, is in her senior year of college. She is a Faith Academy graduate and is currently working toward obtaining a medical degree.

I have been extremely blessed with Godly children. They have seen and experienced firsthand what it means to walk by faith; and I know that my Mom was a tremendous example to them. I know that the things they have learned about trusting the Lord and walking by faith will remain with them forever. My children are truly my *"reward"*. (Psalm 127:3)

Chapter Thirty

"Come On, Tony! It's Time To Move Up!"

∽

On June 5th, 1989, Mom went on to be with the Lord. Four days later, Dad joined her. Just as it was in their lives, Mom led the way and charted the course, and Dad simply followed. I can just imagine Mom going on, forging ahead with her pioneering spirit and calling to Dad, *"Come on, Tony! It's time to move up!"*

About two weeks after they had passed away, Rocco had a dream. In this dream, he was walking out of his church after service. Everyone else had already left and gone home; but as he walked out the door, he saw Mom and Dad standing on the steps. They were in their early thirties. Mom had long, beautiful hair again; and Dad was dressed sharply.

Rocco was very surprised to see them and

said, *"Mom! Dad! What are you doing here?"*
They said, *"Well, we came to visit you because
we want you to tell everyone in the church how
well we are...how wonderful we are!"* Rocco
said that the church was over and everyone
had already gone home; and Mom replied, *"So
let's walk to their houses and tell them."* Rock
suggested that they drive, but Mom insisted
that they could walk. Rocco was so surprised
by this, because Mom had never liked to walk.
And she hated the wind! If it was even slightly
windy out, she would stay home. But here she
was in this dream, wanting to go for a walk.
Rock argue with her, *"Mom, it's windy!"* And
she said to him, *"It's beautiful out! I love the
wind!"*

At this point, Rock realized that Mom and
Dad were speaking perfectly. They didn't have
their broken English accents anymore! Rock
also thought of the picture he had in his office
of them in their seventies, just before they had
died. And he was so overwhelmed with how
beautiful Mom looked standing before him in
this dream.

They started to walk, and Rocco asked
Mom to tell him about Jesus. *"Oh! When Jesus
come near your house, you know it! You know*

when He's nearby!" Then she said, *"Did you know that Jesus likes sports? He likes all kinds of sports."* Rock was amazed!

Mom never talked about sports! Rock doesn't even remember ever hearing Mom use the word "sports" before, and there she was, with her long black hair blowing in the wind, telling him that Jesus likes sports! Rock couldn't get over it! He was thinking to himself, *"Here she—likes to walk, doesn't mind the wind, and is talking about how wonderful it is that Jesus loves sports!"*

When he woke up from the dream, Rocco was so overwhelmed with how beautiful Mom looked. He went into his office at the church, and put away the picture he had on his desk of Mom and Dad in their seventies. He couldn't look at it because he knew that it wasn't real anymore.

That dream that Rocco had was an encouragement to us all. We knew that Mom and Dad were with the Lord, and it gave us a continued peace that everything would be alright.

Chapter Thirty-one

GOD'S FAITHFULNESS CONTINUES

∽

Mom and Dad's "graduation" to going to be with the Lord did not occur until we, their children, were all established in the Word of God and in the plans that God had for us. Ministries had grown, families were settled, and patterns of growth and prosperity were set. Today, we forge ahead as a family, as a pioneering group of people in the Body of Christ, operating together to do the mighty and honorable work of the Lord.

Mom and Dad had taught us to stand in the face of difficulty and trust the Lord. Mom's example of tenacity taught us to believe God for ourselves. Her example of endurance and persistent trust in God's faithfulness to perform on our behalf laid the foundation of our faith.

Mom and Dad sowed, and we reaped. We reaped the blessings of God on our lives. We reaped the wonderful benefit of a tight-knit family, bound together by a mutual faith in God. We reaped the faith to believe what God says, in spite of the circumstances. We reaped the lesson of the power of prayer.

Now we, too, are sowing. We are sowing seeds of prayer and of faith for our family, and we know that they will reap just as we have. *"Do not be deceived, God is not mocked; for whatever a man sows, this he will also reap... and let us not lose heart in doing good, for in due time we shall reap if we do not grow weary."* (Galatians 6:7,9)

I am blessed to have come from such a family, with a Mom who ever prayed for us, and a Dad who ever worked to provide for us. God truly showed Himself faithful to us, and I know that He will continue to prove His faithfulness. *"Because of the Lord's great love we are not consumed, for His compassions never fail. They are new every morning; great is your faithfulness."* (Lamentations 3:22-23)

My prayer is that this book has encouraged you, has given you hope, and has helped you to trust the Lord more. *"Teach My people to trust Me and to walk by faith."* I pray that you have learned what it means to "walk by faith" by reading of my "faith walking" mother. May her story inspire you to press on, to step out and do what God is calling you to do. He will be weigh you every step of the way. He will not leave you stranded. *"Never will I leave you; never will I forsake you"* is His promise (Hebrews 13:5), and, as I always say, *"You fail? Impossible!"*

Chapter Thirty-two

TODAY IS THE DAY OF SALVATION

∽∾

If you have never made the decision to follow Christ, inviting Him to be your Lord and Savior, now is the time. The Bible tells us in Roman 3:23 that *"all have sinned and fall short of the glory of God."* Each one of us has sinned. Each one of us has fallen short of God's glory. But the Bible also tells us that *"if we confess our sins, He is faithful and just and will forgive us our sins, and to cleanse us from all unrighteousness."* (I John 1:9) *"Whosoever shall call upon the name of the Lord shall be saved."* (Romans 10:13) Jesus is faithful to receive you the moment you ask Him to come into your heart.

Salvation is a gift of God's grace. *"For it is by grace you have been saved, through faith— and this not from yourselves, it is the gift of God —not by works, so that no one can boast."* (Ephesians 2:8-9) There is nothing we could ever do to earn salvation. No amount of good works will ever be enough. A sacrifice for our sin is required in order that we might be able to commune (have a relationship) with God. Jesus was that sacrifice. He was 100% God and 100% man, and He lived a perfect life. He died on the cross to pay the penalty for our sins. He was our perfect sacrifice. Three days later, Jesus rose from the dead. He conquered death, hell, and the grave; and He now offers life unto you. John 10:10 says that Jesus came that we might *"have life, and have it to the full."*

Romans 10:9 tell us, *"that if you confess with your mouth, 'Jesus is Lord,' and believe in your heart that God raised Him from the dead, you will be saved."* If you would like to make the decision to follow Jesus, to give God your all, and to serve Him with all of your heart, mind, and strength, pray this prayer with me:

"Father, I come before you in Jesus' Name. I ask you to forgive me of all my sin. I recognize that I have done wrong and that I have fallen short in many areas. You said in Your Word that You would be faithful and just to forgive me, so right now I receive Your forgiveness. I believe that You sent

Your Son Jesus to die on the cross for me, and that on the third day You raised Him from the dead. I confess Jesus as my Lord, and I surrender all of myself to You. I will love You and serve You with all my heart, soul, and might. Thank You, Lord, for loving me and for receiving me as Your child. I believe that by Your grace, through faith, I am now saved. Thank you, Father. In Jesus' Name I pray. Amen."

If you just prayed this prayer, please write us and let us know; and we will send you some material to help you in your new walk with God. If you ever are in need of prayer, feel free to contact us. We are here to serve you.

God bless you!

In His love,

Pastor Dan Cotrone

The Village of Faith Church
1070 Portion Road
Farmingville, NY 11738
516-696-LOVE